TABLE OF CONTENTS

KYLEE TURNER PITTMAN

Discovering TRUTH Daily

A 30-DAY DEVOTIONAL

PREFACE
First Thing's First

If you have not accepted Jesus as your personal Lord & Savior, I would love to share the Good News with you.

When the first humans were formed by God (Adam & Eve), they lived with God without any separation. But they were given a choice (i.e., our free will), and they chose to follow their sinful nature and the temptation of the enemy into disobeying God. This brought sin into the world, causing separation between people and God. Our sin could and *should* keep us eternally separate from God, *but* God loved us and wanted to be close to us so much so that He sent His One and Only Son, Jesus Christ, to earth to die for our sins.

Jesus was born a human and lived a perfect life here on earth so when the time came, He could be the perfect sacrifice to cover all of our sins forever. He died a horrific death to be that bridge that closed the gap between us and God that sin had caused. But that's not where the story ends. God then raised Jesus from the dead, declaring victory over all things, including death, from now until forever.

That's why we, through Jesus, can declare victory over death and sin and look forward to spending eternity with God in Heaven. All we have to do is accept the salvation that we have freely been given by accepting Jesus as our Lord and Savior and believing that God raised Him from the dead.

If you openly declare that Jesus is Lord and believe in your heart that God raised him from the dead, you will be saved. For it is by believing in your heart that you are made right with God, and it is by openly declaring your faith that you are saved.
Romans 10:9-10 (NLT)

You have a purpose. God has a plan for your life. You are never alone and never forgotten about. He knows you by name and wants a relationship with you.

. . . .

If you believe in the message of Jesus and would like to receive this free gift of eternal life, you can say this salvation prayer:

Father God, thank You for sending Your Son, Jesus, to die on the cross for my sins and raising Him to life, conquering death once and for all. I ask for forgiveness for all of my sins. I know that I'm a sinner in need of a Savior and that Savior is Jesus Christ. I declare Jesus as my Lord and my Savior, and I ask that You come into my life and use me to further Your Kingdom here on earth, as I am on my way to my home in Heaven with You.
In Jesus' name, Amen.

. . . .

If you have questions about salvation, I encourage you to read John 3:16-18, Ephesians 2:1-10, 2 Corinthians 5:21, Romans 6, and Romans 8.
You can also reach out to me at
www.discovertruthwithkylee.com.

SECTION 1

BREAKTHROUGH

Bringing freedom from the worry, fear, anxiety, and other things that are holding you back from living out God's plan

Day 1: Freedom in Forgiveness

*Get rid of all bitterness, rage, anger, harsh words, and slander,
as well as all types of evil behavior. Instead, be kind to each
other, tenderhearted, forgiving one another, just as God
through Christ has forgiven you.*
Ephesians 4:31-32 (NLT)

When we really put into perspective how merciful God chooses to be to us, it's hard *not* to forgive others. I remember when I was around ten years old, and my friend really hurt my feelings. I don't recall exactly what happened, but I'm sure we can imagine the kind of things ten-year-olds get upset over. And I *refused* to forgive her because she didn't tell me she was "sorry". I actually remember convincing myself that I didn't *have* to forgive her because she didn't ask for my forgiveness. I'm sure the circumstances are different, but I'd guess a lot of us hold on to bitterness because of this same reason. But get this: As Jesus was being put to death on the cross so we could experience freedom in forgiveness, He said to God, "Father, forgive them, for they don't know what they are doing" (Luke 23:34). Jesus actually asked God for His enemies' forgiveness <u>on their behalf</u>, as He was dying *because* of them. And if Jesus was able to forgive His murderers *and* plead their case to God as He was being executed *because* of them, we should forgive those who wrong us even if they haven't asked for it.

What bitterness or unforgiveness are you holding on to?
Why are you having trouble forgiving?

____

____

Just as God has forgiven us, we are told to forgive others. In fact, the Bible actually goes as far as telling us that if we *don't* forgive others, we ourselves won't be forgiven by God (Matthew 6:15). I don't believe this is meant to scare us into forgiving, but rather to push us into experiencing the freedom that comes from letting go of the unforgiveness we're holding on to.

Today's Prayer:
God,
Thank You for loving me so much that You choose to forgive me. Help me to follow Your example and give forgiveness to anyone I'm holding it back from. Guide me in love and let those around me see the freedom that comes from forgiving others.
In Jesus' name, Amen.

Notes:____

____

____

____

Day 2: Transformation Leads to Revelation

Don't copy the behavior and customs of this world, but let God transform you into a new person by changing the way you think. Then you will learn to know God's will for you, which is good and pleasing and perfect.
Romans 12:2 (NLT)

It all starts with our thoughts. We have to renew our mind in order to discover God's will for us. When we set our thoughts on the things of God, our actions and faith will follow. But this also goes the other way. In times that I personally feel anxious or worried, I notice that I'm letting myself dwell on thoughts of fear and "what-ifs" or am constantly reminding myself that I feel anxious. If I change my focus to thoughts of peace and contentment, my feelings begin to shift. Your feelings follow the leading of your mind. If you keep thinking negatively, your body is going to start feeling those negative emotions which triggers more negative thoughts, and it becomes a continuous cycle. We have to step in and <u>stop the cycle</u>. What I find remarkable about this scripture is that it literally gives us the key to discerning what God's will is in our lives: **changing the way we think**. Your transformation leads to this revelation. When we begin to think like Jesus, by studying God's Word and discovering who He is and what was important to Him during His life on earth, He can begin to show you what His purpose for your life is.

Read Philippians 4:8:
Fix your thoughts on what is true, and honorable, and right, and pure, and lovely, and admirable. Think about things that are excellent and worthy of praise.

Question:
What can you make a conscious effort to focus on when you find yourself letting harmful thoughts creep in?

____

____

When you have negative, fearful, or anxiety-driven thoughts, immediately replace them with a thought focused on Truth. Write down scriptures of promises that you can remind yourself, as you journey to transforming your mind and living out your purpose.

Today's Prayer:
God,
Help renew my mind to focus on the things of Philippians 4:8, and forgive me when I fail. When my thoughts are headed in the wrong direction, help me redirect them to Your Truth. Through this transformation, begin to show me the revelation of the purpose You have for my life.
In Jesus' name, Amen.

Notes:_________________________________

____

Day 3: Facing Rejection

He came into the very world he created, but the world didn't recognize him. He came to his own people, and even they rejected him.
John 1:10-11 (NLT)

This verse continues to stun me every time I read it. The very beings that were created by God, through the power of Jesus Christ, rejected, despised, and humiliated Him. I'm sure we can all recall a time where we felt excluded or forgotten about. I've opened social media before just to see that all of my friends were hanging out together without me. Maybe, as a parent, you have teenage kids who are all of a sudden embarrassed by you and have forgotten all that you've done and sacrificed for them… Can you imagine how Jesus must have felt when He was shut out by the very people He had come to rescue? The hope we can find in this verse is through the realization that Jesus himself went through **and conquered** this worldly rejection. It's great to see Jesus as the powerful, perfect Son of God, but it's also important to understand He came to earth as a lowly carpenter who faced a lot of the same temptations and trials that we face. He felt the betrayal of a friend He loved. He experienced being an outcast and was made fun of for who He was and what He believed. He felt the rejection of people He came to save. He knew the grief from losing a loved one to sickness. He felt the frustration from people not believing what He was saying even though He knew it was the Truth. Jesus relates to you. He gets it. And He also overcame it all and offers that same boldness and perseverance to each of us through Himself.

Question:
Do you ever feel like God doesn't understand what you're going through? After reading this verse, are you more confident that He actually *completely* gets it?

____

____

Not only does He understand, but He *cares*. He loves you and wants to help you through whatever you're facing, so you can be confident bringing your fears, struggles, and afflictions to lay at His feet.

Today's Prayer:
God,
Thank You for leaving Your Kingdom of treasures and glory to be closer to me. Thank You for being my example of faithfulness in the midst of hurt. Help me to overcome the trials and pain I'm facing and to declare victory over it all because of Your sacrifice.
In Jesus' name, Amen.

Notes:____

____

____

____

____

Day 4: Help My Unbelief

*So they brought the boy. But when the evil spirit saw Jesus, it
threw the child into a violent convulsion, and he fell to the
ground, writhing and foaming at the mouth. "How long has
this been happening?" Jesus asked the boy's father. He replied,
"Since he was a little boy. The spirit often throws him into the
fire or into water, trying to kill him. Have mercy on us and help
us, if you can." "What do you mean, 'If I can'?" Jesus
asked. "Anything is possible if a person believes." The father
instantly cried out, "I do believe, but help me overcome my
unbelief!"*
Mark 9:20-24 (NLT)

When we doubt, it doesn't mean we don't have any faith
at all. But it's important to recognize our doubts so we
can overcome them. Charles Spurgeon said, "While men
have no faith, they are unconscious of their unbelief; but,
as soon as they get a little faith, then they begin to be
conscious of the greatness of their unbelief."[1] Realizing
when our faith is lacking is the key to *building* our faith.
Like the boy's father in this passage, we can then go to
God to overcome our unbelief by growing our faith and
removing our doubts. How? One way we can grow our
faith is by learning more about the character of God.
When we read His Word and His promises, we can see
how He has always done what He said He would do, and
He is the same yesterday, today, and forevermore. We
can get rid of our doubt by spending time with God and
personally experiencing His love for us, building our trust
in His willingness to fulfill His promises in our lives. And
when we have trials come our way, we can remind
ourselves that those are the moments that are building

our perseverance as we become more complete and mature in Christ (James 1:2-4).

Question:
In what areas do you struggle with your faith?
(Family restoration? Freedom from addiction? Believing you matter?)

____

____

I encourage you to find Truth in the Bible that corresponds to each area in your life where you're struggling with faith. Put these promises somewhere you will see them every day (mirror, nightstand, counter, etc.), and every time you see them, ask God to help your unbelief in that area and remind yourself that God has already declared victory for you.

Today's Prayer:
God,
Help my unbelief. When I'm struggling in my faith, remind me that Your goodness and unfailing love will pursue me all the days of my life, and Your faithfulness endures to all generations.
In Jesus' name, Amen.

Notes:____

____

Day 5: Surrender the Shame

*So now there is no condemnation for those who belong to
Christ Jesus. And because you belong to him, the power of the
life-giving Spirit has freed you from the power of sin that leads
to death. The law of Moses was unable to save us because of
the weakness of our sinful nature. So God did what the law
could not do. He sent his own Son in a body like the bodies we
sinners have. And in that body God declared an end to sin's
control over us by giving his Son as a sacrifice for our sins. He
did this so that the just requirement of the law would be fully
satisfied for us, who no longer follow our sinful nature but
instead follow the Spirit.*
Romans 8:1-4 (NLT)

We weren't able to obey the 613 commandments in the
law of Moses, so God sent Jesus to fulfill the law on our
behalf. Now we no longer have to carry the shame of our
sins. Once we admit that we're sinners and confess Jesus
as our Savior, we are freed and forgiven of our past. The
Bible tells us that God will forgive our sins and remember
them no more (Jeremiah 31:34). If God Himself doesn't
hold any of our sins against us, why should we continue to
be bound by them? As you read the Bible, you will find
numerous stories of God using people to complete His
work who probably considered themselves "too far
gone". But when we are forgiven, what we've done wrong
in the past is irrelevant, and we can live a new life
glorifying God. So rather than allowing the enemy to
continually use our past to draw us away from accepting
God's grace, let's use our past as a testimony to show
others that there's hope for anyone and everyone. We
can leave our shame at the cross.

How has shame held you back from fulfilling the calling
God has put upon your life?

____

____

The enemy is a liar. He makes us believe that God can't
use us because of our past. But the Truth is, God can use
anyone *despite* their sins. The Bible tells us we are all
sinners and no one sin is greater than another, so no
matter where you've been, you're never out of reach for
the grace of God.

Today's Prayer:
God,
Thank You for sending your Son, Jesus, to erase my sins and
take my shame away. Help me to accept Your mercy and let
go of the shame that is holding me captive. Use my testimony
to help others find the same freedom I have found in You.
In Jesus' name, Amen.

Notes:______________________________________

____

____

____

____

Day 6: Fear is a Liar

Don't be afraid, for I am with you. Don't be discouraged, for I am your God. I will strengthen you and help you. I will hold you up with my victorious right hand.
Isaiah 41:10 (NLT)

In order to overcome our fear, we have to replace it with Truth. In this verse, God doesn't just tell us not to fear, but He tells us the Truth of *why we shouldn't* be afraid. He tells us that we don't have to fear *because* He is with us. I've noticed in my own life that the enemy likes to use a tactic of whispering "half-truths" so they actually sound believable, especially when I'm not spending time in the Word. Thus, the only way we can break free of fear from this method of the enemy is to be able to identify the subtle lies. The way to do that is by knowing *Truth* and by spending time in the Word which *is* Truth so you can have that discernment between Truth and lies. For example, fear will tell you that you could fail. But Truth will tell us that we don't have to be afraid of failing because God will hold us up (Psalm 37:23-24). Fear will tell you that you're not good enough, whereas Truth will tell us that we *all* fall short of the glory of God but have been made right in His sight through our faith in Jesus (Romans 3:22-24). Fear will tell you that your health is failing. But Truth will tell us that by the stripes of Jesus, we are healed (Isaiah 53:5). For every fear we have, there is Truth that shows why fear is a liar. We just have to know that Truth and declare it over our lives. There's a song that I love by Zach Williams called "Fear is a Liar"[2] and part of the chorus speaks on fear robbing you of your rest and happiness, and that is exactly what fear does. It takes away the peace that God has given us (John 14:27).

Let's call out the lies before they can cause fear and
apprehension in our lives.

Question:
What lie has the enemy used to cause fear in your life
recently? What's the Truth that disproves this lie?

____

____

When you feel like fear has a grip on you, I encourage you
to write down the lies the enemy is using to make you
fearful and then search the Word of God for the Truth
that sets you free from those lies and can restore your
peace.

Today's Prayer:
God,
Thank You that no matter what lies the enemy tells me, I can
trust and stand upon Your Truth. Please reveal to me the
Truths that can replace the fear in my life and exchange my
unease with peace, knowing that Your Word is always true.
In Jesus' name, Amen.

Notes:_______________________________________

____

____

____

Day 7: Through His Eyes

When they arrived, Samuel took one look at Eliab and thought, "Surely this is the Lord's anointed!" But the Lord said to Samuel, "Don't judge by his appearance or height, for I have rejected him. The Lord doesn't see things the way you see them. People judge by outward appearance, but the Lord looks at the heart."
I Samuel 16:6-7 (NLT)

This scripture is from the story of the prophet, Samuel, who is being led by God to anoint the person that will become the next king of Israel. God sends Samuel to the home of Jesse, who has eight sons, one of which was chosen by God as the next king. Verse 6 shows us that Samuel did what most of us do, even unknowingly: He immediately made a judgment based on what the son looked like. He believed that Eliab was going to be the chosen king simply because of the way he looked, and <u>he was wrong</u>. It's so encouraging to me that God doesn't determine our worth or purpose the way the world does. The world may say you're not young enough, pretty enough, smart enough, or skinny enough to be what you dream of being or achieve the goals you have set for yourself. But God chose the youngest, most unlikely son to defeat a giant that was way bigger than him and become a king, leading a nation. So next time you let doubt creep in or you take what the world says about your appearance seriously, remember that God's purpose for your life isn't determined by the way you look but by the <u>heart you have</u>. You have been fearfully and wonderfully made, beautiful in God's sight, for a reason, no matter what the world may tell you.

Question:
After reading about how God sees people, if you could look at yourself through the eyes of God, what do you think you would see? Does this match what you see when looking at yourself in the mirror?

____

____

How can we stop judging others based on their appearance when we can't even see past our own insecurities? Practice speaking encouragement over yourself, rather than constantly focusing on your flaws. *"I am kind." "I am a good listener." "I am smart." "I am helpful."*

Today's Prayer:
God,
Help me to see myself through Your eyes, ignoring what the world thinks based on how my appearance fits into their standards. Forgive me when I am quick to judge others. Give me eyes to see them the way You see them, not judging them based on what they look like but instead seeing their heart.
In Jesus' name, Amen.

Notes:_______________________________________

____

____

SECTION 2

DISCOVERY

Leading you to find that God has a specific purpose for your life that can have an impact on your own eternity and the eternity of others

Day 8: Righteousness Follows Relationship

I ask you again, does God give you the Holy Spirit and work miracles among you because you obey the law? Of course not! It is because you believe the message you heard about Christ. In the same way, "Abraham believed God, and God counted him as righteous because of his faith." The real children of Abraham, then, are those who put their faith in God.
Galatians 3:5-7 (NLT)

We aren't saved by our works but by our faith in God. I used to be caught up in doing everything right and checking the boxes of what I thought made me a "good Christian" because I figured that's what would make me close to God. But I realized that I had it backwards. <u>Righteousness follows relationship</u>.
Building a relationship with God and spending time with Him will *cause* you to seek after righteousness. Rather than just following rules, you'll actually desire to live a righteous life. And with that, comes freedom. You'll no longer feel bound by your faith but rather *freed* by it, as you choose to become more and more like Jesus. If you read about the faith of Abraham that's referenced in this passage, you'll learn that he had a lot of room and a lot of time to doubt God and to give up on His promises. But by having faith that God was who He said He was, a God who doesn't lie (Hebrews 6:18) and has good planned for us (Romans 8:28), he was able to see God's promises play out in his life.

Are you following rules because you desire righteousness, or are you trying to "earn" your salvation?

____

____

If you treat your relationship with God like a checklist, it'll always feel like a chore. Once you start chasing after closeness with God, you'll begin to experience the freedom that comes with knowing God and having faith in who He is.

Today's Prayer:

God,

Thank You for wanting a relationship with me. Teach me more about who You are so I can build my faith and let that lead my life. Help me to experience the freedom that comes with believing in You, rather than feeling constrained by just trying to follow a set of rules and not realizing the purpose.
In Jesus' name, Amen.

Notes:_____________________________________

____

____

____

____

Day 9: Purpose in the Wilderness

John grew up and became strong in spirit. And he lived in the wilderness until he began his public ministry to Israel.
Luke 1:80 (NLT)
The Spirit then compelled Jesus to go into the wilderness, where he was tempted by Satan for forty days. He was out among the wild animals, and angels took care of him.
Mark 1:12-13 (NLT)

The season you're in may feel like you're living in the wilderness. You may feel alone, isolated, or like nothing is going your way. But what if we took advantage of that season and looked at the growth that happened for John the Baptist and Jesus while they were in the wilderness? John the Baptist actually lived in the wilderness before starting his teaching in Israel. It was *in the wilderness* that John actually received a message from God (Luke 3:2) and began his ministry, which made a way for the coming of Jesus. For Jesus himself, the Holy Spirit led Him to the wilderness, where His experience wasn't easy. He fasted for 40 days there, and Satan came and tempted Him three times. But He wasn't alone. The Bible tells us that angels came and took care of Him. Two key takeaways from these wilderness experiences are:
1) There's a purpose for the wilderness, and 2) you're not alone in the wilderness. It brings growth, spiritual strength, and preparation so you can be successful in what's to come. And even when you feel like you're in the middle of nowhere, all alone, God and His angels are there with you. Appreciate the season you're in, and take advantage of the opportunity you have to learn and grow before you leave.

Question:
How can you take advantage of the season you're in?

____

____

If you feel like you're in the wilderness right now, use your free time to grow in your faith, knowledge, and relationship with God. If you're on the opposite end and feel like you're in the middle of the ocean during a raging storm, focus on realigning your priorities and appreciating the opportunities and memories God is giving you.

Today's Prayer:
God,
I'm thankful for every season that draws me closer to You. Help me to honor You in every circumstance and trust Your timing for what's to come. Give me hope and strength to get through the wilderness or the chaos and reach my purpose. In Jesus' name, Amen.

Notes:_______________________________________

____

____

____

____

Day 10: Preparing for Hibernation

After seeing him, the shepherds told everyone what had happened and what the angel had said to them about this child. All who heard the shepherds' story were astonished, but Mary kept all these things in her heart and thought about them often.
Luke 2:17-19 (NLT)

As you probably know, when winter is coming, many animals have to prepare for hibernation. They have to consume extra food so their bodies have enough fat to live off of when they go into hibernation for the winter. If these animals don't store enough fat in their bodies for the winter months, they won't survive. We, as people, go through different seasons in our spiritual lives, as well. Sometimes we experience the joy and warmth of summer. Other times, we see the growth and hope of spring or the awe and breeze of fall. But there are also times when we go through the dark and cold of winter. We feel alone, sad, hungry for more. Mary didn't know it yet, but her winter was coming: when her baby boy would be crucified unjustifiably, and she wouldn't be able to do anything to protect Him. She probably didn't realize it at the time, but she was going to need the hope of these moments she stored in her heart where she could be reminded of the wonders and miracles of Jesus and the promises upon His life. In our times of joy, life, and closeness to God, we also need to store those memories of His goodness in our hearts. That way, when we reach our spiritual winters, we can remain hopeful that God is, and always will be, faithful and good and that His promises remain true.

Question:
What's something you can hold on to that will give you
hope in the hard times?

____

____

I encourage you to keep a prayer journal with the things
you're believing God for *and* the prayers He's
answered/wonders you've seen Him do in your life. I
started my prayer journal four years ago, and I love going
back and reminding myself of how God has been faithful
to me time and time again.

Today's Prayer:
God,
Thank You for being with me in every season of my life. Help
me to be reminded of Your goodness and hold on to what
You've done for me so I can remain hopeful even as I walk
through the winters.
In Jesus' name, Amen.

Notes:____

____

____

____

____

Day 11: Your Heart's Desires

Take delight in the Lord, and he will give you your heart's desires.
Psalm 37:4 (NLT)

When my husband proposed to me, it was exactly like I had dreamed about and hoped for. I remember telling my mom right after it happened, "If I could have planned my own proposal, this would have been it." And she simply replied to me, quoting this scripture, "Well, God gives you the desires of your heart." And that was so encouraging and exciting to me. God loves us, and as cliché as it sounds, He wants our dreams to come true as long as they follow His will. Matthew 7:11 says, "So if you sinful people know how to give good gifts to your children, how much more will your heavenly Father give good gifts to those who ask him". If you have a kid, think about them for a minute. And if you don't have any kids, think about your sibling, best friend, or significant other. Don't you wish you could give them everything they ever wanted and make all of their wildest dreams come true? You want that for them because you love them and want to see them smile and their eyes light up. That love you have for them comes from God and is just a glimmer of the love that He has for *you*. When you feel like no one is in your corner or cheering you on, remember this love that He has for you. Remember that He wants you to succeed and wants you to achieve your goals and chase your dreams. He put that motivation and passion inside of us for a reason, and we can use it to do powerful things for the Kingdom of God when we align it with His will.

Question:
Do you believe that God wants good for you? If not, why
is this hard for you to believe?

____

____

God gave us passions and dreams for a reason. He has a
plan and purpose for your dreams to be used in a way
that can advance His Kingdom. We just have to spend
time with Him and follow His lead so He can make our
dreams come true, bringing glory to His Name.

Today's Prayer:
God,
Thank You for giving me dreams and desires, and thank You
for caring about me so much that You care about those things,
too. Use my dreams to further Your Kingdom and bring glory
to Your name.
In Jesus' name, Amen.

Notes:____

____

____

____

____

Day 12: Purpose in the Pain

The jailer called for lights and ran to the dungeon and fell down trembling before Paul and Silas. Then he brought them out and asked, "Sirs, what must I do to be saved?" They replied, "Believe in the Lord Jesus and you will be saved, along with everyone in your household." And they shared the word of the Lord with him and with all who lived in his household. Even at that hour of the night, the jailer cared for them and washed their wounds. Then he and everyone in his household were immediately baptized.
Acts 16:29-33 (NLT)

As they were traveling to different places, preaching the Gospel, Paul and Silas were thrown into jail. When we hear Bible stories, I think we sometimes subconsciously categorize them as if they are fictional stories and don't actually grasp them as actual history. So, I want you to take a minute to think about how you would feel being thrown into prison for obeying God and preaching His Word. Personally, I'm sure I would feel scared and angry. But if Paul and Silas felt this way, they didn't show it in scripture. They actually spent that night praying and praising God, and as you read the story, you'll see that their imprisonment leads to the jailer and the jailer's family accepting Jesus and being baptized. It's hard to understand the purpose of our pain as we're enduring it, but Romans 8:28 promises us that it is used for good, and this passage is the perfect example. If Paul and Silas were never put into prison, that jailer and his family might never have accepted their salvation in Jesus. Our earthly pain and trials are only temporary, and they can be used to have an everlasting impact on someone's eternity.

Question:
Have you ever gone through something and then realized,
afterwards, the good that came from it?

____

____

God is all-knowing, and we are not. So many times, we
don't realize the reason He allows things to happen in our
life. Knowing that His ways are higher, let's take Paul and
Silas' example of trusting in God's plan, even through our
trials.

Today's Prayer:
God,
*Thank You that there's always a bigger and better plan that
You have prepared. Help me to see the purpose in my pain
and to trust that Your way is better than my own. I pray
Romans 8:28 over my life and am thankful for this promise.
In Jesus' name, Amen.*

Notes:____

____

____

____

Day 13: Life After Death

Jesus told her, "I am the resurrection and the life. Anyone who believes in me will live, even after dying. Everyone who lives in me and believes in me will never ever die..."
John 11:25-26 (NLT)

Are you afraid to die? Death is a fear for many people, and I believe that's for two reasons:
1. The person afraid doesn't have faith in life after our earthly bodies die. And/or 2. They don't have any experience with dying. We ourselves don't know what dying is like and others around us can't tell us what it's like, so this fear of the unknown causes the fear of death. However, the Bible can erase both of those reasons to be afraid of death for us. 1. We can rest assured in the promise that God gives eternal life to those who believe Jesus is Lord (read Romans 10:9-10 for more detail). And not just any ordinary life, but life filled with joy, without any more death, pain, or sorrow (Revelation 21:4). The kind of life that we dream about. We can look forward to this eternal life after our earthly bodies die when we're confident in the salvation God has freely given those who accept it. 2. We may not have firsthand experience with dying, but the Bible tells us what it'll be like. It describes the beauty of our new home (Revelation 22) and how all of our questions will be answered (1 Corinthians 13:12). It tells us that when we die on earth, we enter our real home, Heaven, and begin our life with our Father and brothers and sisters in Christ, where Jesus has prepared a place for us (John 14:2). When we have accepted our salvation in Christ, earthly death is nothing to be afraid of because it's just the start of our true life.

Question:
Are you afraid to die? If so, why? What in the Bible can build your confidence in trusting God with your life, even after your earthly body dies?

____

____

God created us to be close with Him. We are only separated because of sin, but through humanly death, we can actually be united with God and Christ like we were designed to be.

Today's Prayer:
God,
Thank You for Your gift of eternal life. Help me to not fear death but have faith in Your promises. I confess Jesus as my personal Lord and Savior and believe You rose Him from the dead after He died on the cross for my sins and for my gift of eternity. Help me to be confident in my salvation and live every day following Your plan and looking forward to one day meeting You face to face.
In Jesus' name, Amen.

Notes:_______________________________________

____

____

____

Day 14: More Than Your Soul

*And what do you benefit if you gain the whole world but lose
your own soul? Is anything worth more than your soul?*
Matthew 16:26 (NLT)

Let's answer those questions: 1. By changing who you are
to please the world, you may gain money, fame, and
attention, but in trade for your soul, you'll end up missing
out on your purpose and losing out on eternity with
Jesus. Putting it into perspective, the second question is
easy to answer: "No way."
But it's not as easy to live as though we really believe that.
Most, if not all, of us have a desire to be liked and/or
accepted, which can lead us to change who we are and
who we were created to be to please others. And living in
a social media era makes it even more difficult. We're
constantly judged and "liked" based on what we post,
while also being able to easily compare ourselves to
others who may seem prettier, smarter, in better shape,
or more popular than us. Being even a little invested in
those things can cause us to change who we are to mimic
others or to become who we think others want us to be.
In order to change this, I think it's important to
understand two verses: Ephesians 2:10 and John 15:19.
We were specifically designed by God and given a
purpose here on earth. With that purpose, there's a
reason we may not fit in or be liked by everyone, and
that's because we are called to live *in* the world but not *of*
the world.

Question:
Do you value the world's opinion higher than God's? If so,
why?

____

____

What the world can offer us is temporary, but what God
offers us is eternal. When you find yourself living by the
world's standards, remind yourself that nothing is worth
more than your soul.

Today's Prayer:
God,
Thank You for uniquely designing me with a specific purpose.
Help me to value Your opinion only and make the well-being of
my soul and the souls around me my priority in life.
In Jesus' name, Amen.

Notes:____

____

____

____

____

SECTION 3

ATTAINMENT

Encouraging you to intentionally step into that purpose, where you can live a fulfilled and joyful life

Day 15: Try it His Way

Then, calling the crowd to join his disciples, he said, "If any of you wants to be my follower, you must give up your own way, take up your cross, and follow me. If you try to hang on to your life, you will lose it. But if you give up your life for my sake and for the sake of the Good News, you will save it."
Mark 8:34-35 (NLT)

If you've ever jumped off a rope swing, you probably understand the importance of letting go. I've seen so many people hold on tight as they swing out, afraid to let go of the rope, only to get stuck hanging over the shallow end of the water, unable to get back to the shore or swing out further. When we try to hold on to our own life and don't let go and trust God with it, we miss out on the freedom and joy that comes from jumping. We get stuck in a life that's missing purpose, as we're just hanging there, becoming weaker and weaker.

Sometimes we think we're doing it right – holding on tight until the perfect moment, at the perfect time where we say we'll finally let go. But in doing that, we can confuse the *right* way with *our own* way. This verse tells us that if we try to keep our life our own way, by holding on tight to what *we* want and how *we* think things should go, we'll actually miss out on the life we're supposed to be living. We will miss out on the things God has for us and who He created us to be. But if we will let go of our way and take up our cross by surrendering to God and His plan, we can actually receive true freedom and live out our purpose.

Question:
What's something you're holding on to that's keeping you
from giving your all to God?
(Ex: fear, addictions, a bad relationship, your need to have
control, etc.)

____

____

If you want to live your life the way God created you to
live it, it's time to let go of what you're holding on to and
cling on to the promises of God. He works all things for
the good of those who love Him (Romans 8:28).

Today's Prayer:
God,
*Thank You for being my example of letting go in order to save.
Thank You for letting go of Your Son, Jesus, so He could come
into the world to save me. Help me to respond by letting go of
my way, picking up my cross, and following after You. Have
Your way in and through my life.
In Jesus' name, Amen.*

Notes:_______________________________________

____

____

____

Day 16: All for Something

So let's not get tired of doing what is good. At just the right time we will reap a harvest of blessing if we don't give up. Therefore, whenever we have the opportunity, we should do good to everyone—especially to those in the family of faith.
Galatians 6:9-10 (NLT)

Do you ever feel like you're doing things right, but everything is still going wrong? Just today, I worked really hard and spent hours and hours on something, just to be told that I needed to redo it. I was frustrated and annoyed because I thought I did everything the right way, and it ended up feeling like it was all for nothing. But then I read this scripture and realized that doing good is never all for nothing. Even without seeing a harvest immediately, doing good teaches discipline, helps others see the love of Jesus, and fixates your heart and attitude on what's important. Next time you're debating on whether doing the right thing is worth it, read this promise and know that *it is.* Your blessing is promised if you don't give up. Until then, look around at the effect you're having on others by choosing to do good. Look at the smile you caused on someone else's face by giving them a compliment. Notice your child treating a new friend with kindness because of your example. See that the stranger's day was made because you took the time to have a conversation with them.
It's never all for nothing. It's something that just may change everything.

Question:
When do you have the toughest time choosing to do good? (When you're not seeing the benefit? When someone has wronged you?)

____

____

Make the decision today to choose good even when it feels like you're not getting it in return. You can't control how other people act or respond, but you can control how *you* do.

Today's Prayer:
God,
Thank You for Your promise of blessing if I don't give up in doing good. Help me to choose good even when it seems difficult or unrewarding. Give me opportunities, today, that I can show someone else the love of Jesus. Thank You for making doing good always worth it in the end.
In Jesus' name, Amen.

Notes:_______________________________________

____

____

____

____

Day 17: Heart Check

"If you are faithful in little things, you will be faithful in large ones. But if you are dishonest in little things, you won't be honest with greater responsibilities."
Luke 16:10 (NLT)

This scripture reminds me of the question: "What do you do when no one's looking?" When we tell white lies or try to hide small things, we most likely don't think we're going to get caught. And it's in these moments where we can see our true heart and motives come out. This also applies to where God places us at different points in our life. If we're working somewhere we don't want to be, on our way to where we *do* want to be, and we use that time to be lazy or work haphazardly, it shows the ungratefulness or bitterness in our heart, which doesn't just change with a new job title. Taking a bitter or ungrateful heart to bigger responsibility doesn't make you better, it only widens the sphere of influence you have. When you go from the bottom to the top or little things to big things, <u>your character goes with you</u>, so we have to make sure we have the heart of God even in the little things before we can be entrusted with greater responsibility.

Work willingly at whatever you do, as though you were working for the Lord rather than for people.
Colossians 3:23 (NLT)

Are you honest in the little things or only when you see it as a big deal?

____

____

Test your heart. Are you honest in the little things, even when no one's looking? Maybe you've been waiting on something big to happen in your life, meanwhile God's waiting on a heart change so you can fulfill your purpose in the big things.

Today's Prayer:
God,
Thank You that You always know where and what is best for me. Help me to be honest and hardworking in all circumstances. Give me the ability to see the importance of every opportunity that comes my way, no matter the size. Shift any selfishness and dishonesty in my heart to gratefulness and faithfulness.
In Jesus' name, Amen.

Notes:____

____

____

____

____

Day 18: Feeling Spiritually Superior

"The Pharisee stood by himself and prayed this prayer: 'I thank you, God, that I am not like other people—cheaters, sinners, adulterers. I'm certainly not like that tax collector! I fast twice a week, and I give you a tenth of my income.' But the tax collector stood at a distance and dared not even lift his eyes to heaven as he prayed. Instead, he beat his chest in sorrow, saying, 'O God, be merciful to me, for I am a sinner.' I tell you, this sinner, not the Pharisee, returned home justified before God. For those who exalt themselves will be humbled, and those who humble themselves will be exalted."
Luke 18:11-14 (NLT)

I don't know about you, but when I first read this passage, I thought, "How dare he?" But then I thought a little more and realized that I may not have prayed that Pharisee's same prayer before, but I sure have had that same attitude. When we look down on someone or judge other people for their mistakes, we're revealing that we feel spiritually superior. We are all sinners and all fall short of the glory of God. With no sin being greater than another in God's eyes, we're no better than anyone around us. Once we recognize that, our view of other people and ourselves can change, and God can use us for His glory. When we exalt ourselves, most of the time it's because *we* want the glory of our successes. But when we stay humble and allow God to exalt us in His timing, He gets the glory for the successes He's given us, which can then be used to minister to others. Let's take the attitude of the tax collector, recognizing that we are sinners in need of a Savior and always coming to Jesus with a posture of humility.

Question:
What can you remind yourself when you start to feel
spiritually superior?

____

____

Stay humble and at the right time, God can lift you up for
His glory, and your story can be a testament to others.

Today's Prayer:
God,
Give me eyes to see people the way You see them. Help me to
show others the grace You so mercifully show me. I admit that
I'm a sinner and am no better than any other, so help me to
keep an attitude of humility.
In Jesus' name, Amen.

Notes:____

____

____

____

____

____

Day 19: Passion for a Purpose

God has given each of you a gift from his great variety of spiritual gifts. Use them well to serve one another. Do you have the gift of speaking? Then speak as though God himself were speaking through you. Do you have the gift of helping others? Do it with all the strength and energy that God supplies. Then everything you do will bring glory to God through Jesus Christ. All glory and power to him forever and ever! Amen.
I Peter 4:10-11 (NLT)

I always have had a desire to be a teacher. I have a passion for teaching and for showing the love of Jesus to children. However, I didn't feel led to go to college for education or start my career in teaching. A few months ago, I was thinking about this when God brought to mind my current role in my home church: I am the elementary children's director, which means I spend most of my Sundays in the kids' area, teaching Bible stories, leading worship, and sharing the love of Jesus with the kids. I *am* a teacher–teaching kids even. It might not have happened the way I thought it would, but God gave me my passion of teaching kids for a reason, and I get to use it to serve God and others every week. I believe that God created us with certain passions for a reason, so it's important we use our passions to serve the Kingdom of God. If you read about the life of Saul (aka Paul) in the Bible, you'll see that, at first, **he had his passion right but his mission wrong**. He was using his gift of boldness and speaking to serve the wrong kingdom, but once he got ahold of the Truth and began using his voice to fulfill the purpose God had for him, he completely changed the trajectory of his life and countless others.

Question:
What are you passionate about? How could this be used
to serve God and others?

____

____

Pastor Scott Niemeier often says that "our passions align
with our purpose". God gives us strengths, desires, and
interests intentionally. We just have to make sure we're
using them for God's mission.

Today's Prayer:
God,
Thank You for giving me passions that can be used to fulfill
Your purpose for my life. Show me where I can use my gifts
and interests to serve You and other people.
In Jesus' name, Amen.

Notes:____

____

____

____

____

____

Day 20: Representing Jesus

Imitate God, therefore, in everything you do because you are his dear children. Live a life filled with love, following the example of Christ...
Ephesians 5:1-2 (NLT)

Did you ever get that pep talk from your elementary school teacher before a field trip explaining that everyone needed to be on their best behavior because "you're representing me"? This passage from Paul reminds me of those pep talks. Like my 5th grade teacher, Paul is telling us that we are reflections of Christ, thus he encourages us to live in a way that represents Jesus well. Some people may never read the Bible, go to church, or build a relationship with God, so their only impression of Christ is from believers they encounter, such as us. That's why it's so important that we do our best to represent Jesus well by imitating who He is. But how can we behave like Jesus if we, ourselves, aren't familiar with the character of Christ?

In order to be the best representation of Jesus we can be for others, we have to learn who He is. We can do this by reading His Word and building a relationship with Him. When we read about the life of Jesus, we can learn about how He was compassionate towards others, especially the lost and hurting (Matthew 9:36), He was faithful in prayer (Luke 6:12), He was humble (Philippians 2:5-8), He demonstrated servant leadership (John 13:4-16), He empowered others to fulfill their purpose (Matthew 28:18-20), He was committed to telling others about His Father (Matthew 9:35), and when we listen and take the time to get to know our Savior, we can begin to display His character to others.

Are you a good representation of Jesus to others?
Could people know the character of Christ by knowing
you?

____

____

Some people step away from God solely because of how
they were treated by Christians, which they associated
with who Christ is. While we can't be perfect, we should
continuously aim to become more and more like Jesus
every day, showing His love and kindness to everyone we
encounter.

Today's Prayer:
God,
*Thank You for giving me the honor of representing You. Help
me to not take this responsibility lightly, to mimic the character
of Christ in how I live and how I love others, and to let people
know You just by knowing me.
In Jesus' name, Amen.*

Notes:____

____

____

____

Day 21: Autopilot

So be careful how you live. Don't live like fools, but like those who are wise. Make the most of every opportunity in these evil days. Don't act thoughtlessly, but understand what the Lord wants you to do.
Ephesians 5:15-17 (NLT)

Have you ever caught yourself operating on autopilot? We may think it's not a big deal because we're still doing what needs to get done, but the problem with living on autopilot is the lack of intentionality. You no longer are being intentional in the things you do or conversations you have but are just getting through them so you can move on. What kind of space is that giving the Holy Spirit to move through you? When we aren't intentionally listening for the yearnings of the Holy Spirit and being aware of opportunities that come up to share love or the Word with others, we can miss out on our purpose. Years ago, my family and I went to Altitude Trampoline Park®, and I remember my little brother and I both went to use the restroom. As I opened the door and walked in, I noticed my brother about to follow me right into the women's bathroom. He wasn't really paying attention to anything around him, just walking on autopilot, and he went the wrong way because of it.

When we are "zoned out" or distracted, whether it be by our thoughts, other responsibilities, or even our phone, not only can we miss out on opportunities God has for us, but we can also end up taking the wrong turn. So, it's important we "don't act thoughtlessly" like the scripture says but are intentional and always ready and willing to move when God wants us to.

How can you be more intentional in your actions and conversations with others?

____

____

If David had just been on autopilot when delivering food to his brothers as they were in battle with the Philistines, he could have missed his opportunity to defeat Goliath and bring victory to the Israelites (1Samuel 17). You never know what you're missing when you're on autopilot.

Today's Prayer:
God,
Help me to be intentional in my daily walk. Give me the eyes to see opportunities to share Your love and goodness with others and the ears to listen as You lead me in conversations of Truth and kindness. When I am operating on autopilot, about to miss a chance or take a wrong turn, nudge me in the way I should move.
In Jesus' name, Amen.

Notes:_______________________________________

____

____

____

Day 22: Stalling Your Purpose

Lazy people want much but get little, but those who work hard will prosper.
Proverbs 13:4 (NLT)

Have you ever felt stuck in limbo in life? Like you're in an interim stage, just waiting for the next big thing or breakthrough to happen so you can step into your purpose? I felt like I was at this point recently, and I was thinking about why I am where I am and I'm not where I think I *should* be. And as I started asking God the reason for me being where I was and not somewhere else, I realized that I was the one stalling my own dreams. I have a dream of being a writer/speaker, but at that point in time, I hadn't written in months. I wasn't doing anything to work towards my goals. Whether intentional or not, you may be stalling your own next steps to fulfilling your purpose.
God gave us free will, meaning He doesn't force us into our purpose. We have to *choose* to step into it. I'm not saying we should try to rush God's plan and make it happen in our time, but we do have a part to play. God can give us the dream, talents, and opportunities, and then we should put the work, time, and effort in to see our purpose succeed.
God has a plan for you (Jeremiah 29:11), so if you feel like you're just treading water, keeping your head afloat but not getting anywhere, ask God to show you where you need to work or move to step into the purpose and plan He has for your life. Then, do it.

Question:
How long has it been since you've worked towards the
desires of your heart?

____

____

Take a minute to pray for God to lead you in His
direction, and then do something that contributes to your
goals. Whether that means practicing, learning,
composing, or planning, spend 15 minutes today doing it.

Today's Prayer:
God,
*I ask You to show me the direction You want me to go, help
equip me with what I need to succeed, and give me
opportunities to fulfill the purpose You have for my life. When
I'm feeling stalled, give me the desire to pursue the goals and
dreams You have given me.*
In Jesus' name, Amen.

Notes:____

____

____

____

____

SECTION 4

EXPANSION

Using your freedom and purpose to
help others discover the same for
themselves

Day 23: Out of Your Comfort Zone

One day Naomi said to Ruth, "My daughter, it's time that I found a permanent home for you, so that you will be provided for. Boaz is a close relative of ours, and he's been very kind by letting you gather grain with his young women. Tonight he will be winnowing barley at the threshing floor. Now do as I tell you—take a bath and put on perfume and dress in your nicest clothes. Then go to the threshing floor, but don't let Boaz see you until he has finished eating and drinking. Be sure to notice where he lies down; then go and uncover his feet and lie down there. He will tell you what to do."
"I will do everything you say," Ruth replied.
Ruth 3:1-5 (NLT)

How uncomfortable do you think Ruth felt going and laying at the feet of Boaz, someone she barely knew, uninvited? I don't know about you, but I'm not sure I could have fought my discomfort to do what she did. A few years ago, I had an interview for the job I had been praying for, and at the end of it, I was invited to a tailgate the company was hosting on my school's campus. I was so nervous to go that I actually approached the tailgate, looked in, and walked right past. I called my now husband and told him how I was debating on not going because of how awkward and uncomfortable I felt. He encouraged me to step out of my comfort zone and go, so I worked up the courage and walked in. Immediately, I was welcomed by the few people I had met at my interview. After only a few minutes, I was pulled aside by the head recruiter and offered the position I so badly wanted. I was completely astonished that I almost missed that opportunity, solely because I let discomfort get in the way of God's plan for me. If Ruth would not have pushed past the discomfort, Boaz might not have married her, and she may not have had her son, who would become the grandfather of David. Not everything we are called to do will be in our comfort zone. God pushes us out so that we can grow and reach further. Take a step, even when you feel uncomfortable, and you'll be surprised at the opportunities you're given.

Question:
Are you letting discomfort keep you from the new opportunities God is giving you?

____

____

Today's Prayer:
God,
Thank You for giving me opportunities to grow. Help me to step out of my comfort zone and into the things You have planned for me, knowing You're by my side the entire time. In Jesus' name, Amen.

Notes:_______________________________________

____

____

____

Day 24: His Power Through You

Peter and John went to the Temple one afternoon to take part in the three o'clock prayer service. As they approached the Temple, a man lame from birth was being carried in. Each day he was put beside the Temple gate, the one called the Beautiful Gate, so he could beg from the people going into the Temple. When he saw Peter and John about to enter, he asked them for some money. Peter and John looked at him intently, and Peter said, "Look at us!" The lame man looked at them eagerly, expecting some money. But Peter said, "I don't have any silver or gold for you. But I'll give you what I have. In the name of Jesus Christ the Nazarene, get up and walk!" Then Peter took the lame man by the right hand and helped him up. And as he did, the man's feet and ankles were instantly healed and strengthened. He jumped up, stood on his feet, and began to walk! Then, walking, leaping, and praising God, he went into the Temple with them.
Acts 3:1-8 (NLT)

This is such a cool story to me because it demonstrates that we really do have the power of Jesus in us, and we can use it to perform miracles just like Jesus did Himself. Peter is a great example of having faith that God can work *through* us. Peter didn't pray silently for the man's healing *just in case* it didn't work. He was bold and confident that Jesus would use him to heal this man who had been lame for over 40 years. If you read further in Acts 3, you'll see that Peter then uses this opportunity to give God the glory and share who Jesus is with all of the witnesses. He didn't let this miracle boost his ego and take the credit for it. He knew that God deserved the praise and that using his platform was the perfect opportunity to share the Good News with the crowd of Israelites. Let Peter motivate you to be confident in who Jesus is and who you are in Him, then let His power shine through you so others can learn about the miracle worker you know.

Question:
Do you believe that God could use you to literally heal a lame man? What makes you doubt?

____

____

If you're like me, you may believe this for others but have trouble believing that it's really true for you. If that's the case, I encourage you to read John 14:12-14 and ask God for help believing this for yourself. He is no respecter of persons, and He can use you just as He uses others.

Today's Prayer:
God,
Thank You for choosing me to bring glory to Your name. Help me to honor You in everything You do through me. Give me faith and boldness to call forth healing for the sick, broken, and hurting, which I pray brings others to know You.
In Jesus' name, Amen.

Notes:____

____

____

Day 25: Unashamed

Then they reached Jericho, and as Jesus and his disciples left town, a large crowd followed him. A blind beggar named Bartimaeus (son of Timaeus) was sitting beside the road. When Bartimaeus heard that Jesus of Nazareth was nearby, he began to shout, "Jesus, Son of David, have mercy on me!" "Be quiet!" many of the people yelled at him. But he only shouted louder, "Son of David, have mercy on me!" When Jesus heard him, he stopped and said, "Tell him to come here." So they called the blind man. "Cheer up," they said. "Come on, he's calling you!" Bartimaeus threw aside his coat, jumped up, and came to Jesus. "What do you want me to do for you?" Jesus asked. "My Rabbi," the blind man said, "I want to see!" And Jesus said to him, "Go, for your faith has healed you." Instantly the man could see, and he followed Jesus down the road.
Mark 10:46-52 (NLT)

As followers of Jesus, we're probably going to be told to "be quiet" or get laughed at for what we believe at some point, but I love how Bartimaeus responded. He wasn't too embarrassed or ashamed of His belief in the power of Jesus. In fact, when he was told to "be quiet", he just yelled **louder**. He didn't care if people thought he was crazy; he was persistent in calling out to Jesus for his healing. What if we are like this any time we need healing? What if we call on the name of Jesus with such faith that we don't care who hears or what people think? Furthermore, let's also respond in the way Bartimaeus did *after* Jesus called for him. He jumped up and threw his cloak aside. When Bartimaeus threw this coat, he was leaving, quite possibly, everything he owned behind, trusting his future in the hands of Jesus. That cloak was used to represent him as a beggar, giving him the ability to collect money, but he threw it aside, knowing that he would no longer need it after an encounter with Jesus. We can also have faith that our encounters with Jesus can change our circumstances and give us a hope and future (Jeremiah 29:11).

Question:
Do you have enough faith in Jesus that you don't care what people think? If not, how can you grow your faith?

____

____

Bartimaeus didn't just receive his healing and forget about Jesus. After he received his healing, he began to *follow* Jesus. Let's not forget about what Jesus has done for us (including dying on the cross for our sins), but let's honor His love and sacrifice by following Him.

Today's Prayer:
God,
Thank You for caring and listening to everyone, even if others don't see them as worthy. Help me to be bold about—and proud of—my faith and relationship with You, knowing an encounter with You can change everything. Give me opportunities to share this Truth with others around me.
In Jesus' name, Amen.

Notes:____

Day 26: Genuine Love

Don't just pretend to love others. Really love them. Hate what is wrong. Hold tightly to what is good. Love each other with genuine affection, and take delight in honoring each other.
Romans 12:9-10 (NLT)

God doesn't call us to fake our love for others or just be nice to people. He tells us to *really* love them. This is hard for me because I sometimes feel like me being nice to someone, whether I like them or not, is doing enough. I can choose to show kindness to others, but how can I choose to love someone? This verse gives us great advice for this question: Hate what is wrong. Hate the sin, not the person. We all make mistakes, and there are things about all of us that are unrighteous (that's why we need a Savior). But instead of judging a person based on their sin, we should look for the good in others and hold on to this. We would want the same from them, wouldn't we? Pastor Scott Niemeier says, "We judge ourselves by our intentions, but we judge others by their actions". What if we change that and start giving others the grace and love we expect for ourselves? Jesus led by example in this by eating with sinners and showing love to those that were hated (Mark 2:15-16). He even truly loved those that persecuted Him and showed them mercy with His dying breath (Luke 23:34). We should follow this example and cling to the good in others. This scripture goes on to say how we should "delight in honoring each other". It's not a competition, and we're no better than any other, so we should be glad when we can lift someone else up. Jesus was the Son of God. He could've come to Earth in riches and glory, but He chose to come as a humble servant to others, respecting and honoring His friends *and* enemies. This is our example of genuine love and affection.

Question:
Are you ever fake to others? How can you choose to genuinely love others even when it's hard?

____

____

If you're struggling to truly love someone, start writing out a list of all the good you see in them. Are they kind to strangers? Do they make others feel included? Do they care about their family? When you are having trouble loving them with genuine love, read over this list and remind yourself that we are all sinners, and while God hates sin, He still chooses to truly love us.

Today's Prayer:
God,
Help me to see people the way You see them, hating the sin but loving the person. When I struggle, remind me that You love me despite how many times I fall short of Your glory. Thank You for choosing to see my good and loving me with genuine affection.
In Jesus' name, Amen.

Notes:_____________________________________

____

Day 27: People Focus

"Therefore, go and make disciples of all the nations, baptizing them in the name of the Father and the Son and the Holy Spirit. Teach these new disciples to obey all the commands I have given you. And be sure of this: I am with you always, even to the end of the age."
Matthew 28:19-20 (NLT)

Notice how Jesus didn't call us to only preach the Gospel to those who attend church on Sunday morning. We are called to share the Gospel with *everyone*. This is the Great Commission—the mission Jesus left with us before He physically departed from the earth.

Recently, I was having a difficult time trying to understand how I could make a difference or advance the Kingdom of God when my day job is in the corporate world, analyzing numbers. Then I realized that the task may not have an eternal importance, but *the people do*. You don't have to be working in ministry to fulfill Your purpose of reaching *people*. Actually, those that have jobs outside of the church can reach people that the church might not ever be able to—people that would never step into a church or open an Instagram live and listen to a message. You have the ability to impact people who may never hear the Gospel or be aware of the love of Jesus otherwise. Wherever you are, whatever your day job is, there are people in your path that need to see Jesus through you to change the trajectory of their soul.

Question:
Do you ever lose sight of your calling to reach people?
Do you prioritize getting things done over building
relationships with people?

____

____

Recognizing this can fix your focus. Think about it: If I'm
the very best at completing all of the tasks in my job
description, but I never smile at my coworker or take an
interest in how they're doing, then I'm missing the
opportunities God gave me to reach the lost.

Today's Prayer:
God,
Thank You that I have opportunities to reach people for You,
wherever I am. Help me to focus on people over my tasks and
share the love of Jesus with those You put in my path.
In Jesus' name, Amen.

Notes:____

____

____

____

____

Day 28: Plant the Seed

I planted the seed in your hearts, and Apollos watered it, but it was God who made it grow. It's not important who does the planting, or who does the watering. What's important is that God makes the seed grow.
I Corinthians 3:6-7 (NLT)

Where I went to college, every Tuesday night, they have this event called "Breakaway". It's basically a huge church service where thousands of college students come together on our school's campus. One Tuesday, I really felt the urge to ask one of my friends to come with us. I wasn't sure if he believed in God or not, but I went ahead and invited him. To my surprise, he said yes and joined us that night. But about 30 minutes through praise and worship, I realized that night was worship night and there would be no sermon or message. I was so upset. The one night he came, he wouldn't even hear a message and would probably be bored the whole time just listening to songs. At the end of the night, because it was the last Breakaway of the semester, they had some reflection questions to see how God had moved in our lives. At this point, I was bummed out and regretting that I wasted his one time coming on tonight. That is until they asked everyone to stand who had either accepted Jesus this semester or come back into a relationship with Him. And as I look around the room, watching dozens of people stand, I also see my friend boldly stand up. Come to find out, he had made that decision *that* night at Breakaway. You see, I made the mistake of misunderstanding my role. I wasn't called to "save" my friend. I wasn't called to pick the perfect event with the perfect number of songs and perfect message so that my friend was sure to feel Jesus moving. I was called to just do my part, and let God do the rest. And that's exactly what He did. So next time you feel overwhelmed sharing Jesus with others, remember that all we need to do is plant the seed, and God makes it grow.

Question:
Do you ever do nothing because you feel like you can't do enough? How has your perspective changed?

____

____

When I don't know where to start, I often remind myself: "Just plant the seed".

Today's Prayer:
God,
I'm so grateful that You are always working and moving in people's lives. Help me to understand that it's You, not me, that changes people, so all I have to do is be obedient and then trust that You will do the rest.
In Jesus' name, Amen.

Notes:___________________________________

____

____

Day 29: What's Your Perspective?

So we don't look at the troubles we can see now; rather, we fix our gaze on things that cannot be seen. For the things we see now will soon be gone, but the things we cannot see will last forever.
2 Corinthians 4:18 (NLT)

A couple of years ago, I was sitting at a red light when I looked over to the next lane and saw the car next to me slowly moving *backwards*. I immediately thought "Wow, this person is really backing up when there's a car right behind him?" I was getting ready to honk my horn, when I glanced forward for a second and realized that I was in fact the one slowly moving *forward*, as I wasn't holding the brake down all the way. I immediately laughed out loud, thinking that this is how we are in life a lot of times. Think about it. Have you ever blamed someone else for a situation you got yourself in? Or, have you ever been so focused on the people and things around you that you missed what was right in front of you?
This scripture is talking about focusing on eternal things, rather than the temporary things of this world. Money, fame, beauty—these are all things the world emphasizes as important but won't actually matter to you in 30, 50, or 100 years. When we change our perspective from what the world says matters and fix our eyes forward on eternity, we won't be caught up in trying to "Keep up with the Jones'" or be completely shattered when something doesn't go our way. Rather than trying to constantly fill a void with the newest shoes or latest trends, we can find real fulfillment and purpose as we realize we are actually impacting eternity.

How have you eternally impacted the world? If you don't feel like you have, how can you today?

____

____

We can have an eternal impact every day through showing God's love to others, sharing the Gospel, giving forgiveness to those who have wronged us since we have been forgiven by God, etc. Make it a goal today to purposely do something that can have an eternal impact on someone else's life.

Today's Prayer:
God,
Help me to keep my eyes on You and eternity, rather than the temporary things of the world. Give me a new perspective on the importance of my life, and use me to impact eternity for Your good.
In Jesus' name, Amen.

Notes:___________________________________

____

____

____

____

Day 30: What's the Point?

"But you will receive power when the Holy Spirit comes upon you. And you will be my witnesses, telling people about me everywhere—in Jerusalem, throughout Judea, in Samaria, and to the ends of the earth."
Acts 1:8 (NLT)

Do you ever ask yourself, "What's the point?" whether it be about doing the right thing, working hard, or even living life itself? We can get so caught up in the daily routine of work and responsibilities that we forget the whole point of living in the first place. Before Jesus left this earth and ascended back into Heaven, He said these words, seen in these verses. This is our purpose: to go and tell people about Christ. Our purpose on earth is for eternity. If you just look at the life of Jesus, who is our example, you can find that same purpose lived out. The only difference is the way God has purposed us to do that. Wherever you are, you have an impact on someone around you. Whether you are working in a corporate office, going grocery shopping, or taking your dog for a walk, you can influence someone else's life, and that's the point of you being here. If you're struggling with feeling like your life matters, I encourage you to begin living it the way you were designed to—sharing God's love and kindness with those around you. Not only will it matter to them, but you will actually feel fulfilled and joyful when you understand the point of your life and start living that out. That's what we were designed to do and what our souls crave. If you don't know where to start, ask God to reveal opportunities for you to touch others, as you live out His plan for your life.

Question:
Do you ever feel like there's no point in living? What
makes you think this?

____

____

You matter to someone, but most importantly, you
matter to God. There are so many things that could have
stopped you from being alive today, but here you are.
That is not an accident. You're here for a reason.
(If you need prayer, call the KSBJ Prayer and Care Line at
281-652-5555, open 24/7.)

Today's Prayer:
God,
Thank You for loving me and caring for me, even when I feel
like no one does. Help me to understand the point in living and
find joy in fulfilling Your purpose for my life. Use me to touch
the lives of others and bring them to know Your love and Your
purpose for their own lives.
In Jesus' name, Amen.

Notes:_______________________________________

____

____

____

ACKNOWLEDGEMENTS

To my husband, parents, siblings, family, and friends:
THANK YOU!
Your words of encouragement, support in my goals and dreams, useful tips, and excitement for me mean more than you know. I am so grateful for each and every one of you.

A special shoutout goes to my mom, Courtney, (my self-proclaimed armor-bearer) for the hours you spent editing the devotional, my dad, Brett, for giving the devotional a trial run and providing feedback, my husband, Connor, for encouraging me to chase this dream (even through late nights), and my siblings, Zane, Lexi, Will, and Caitlyn, for your constant support. All of you (+Randi♡) birthed the idea of writing a devotional in the first place, so I wouldn't be here, let alone who I am, without you.

To my readers: Thank you for making my dream a reality. I pray this devotional helped you find freedom, breakthrough, inspiration, peace, and purpose and that you feel encouraged to step in and live out the purpose God has for you, letting go of the things that were holding you back.

And most importantly, I thank God for giving me the passions, giftings, words, and opportunities to serve Him through writing. He is such a mighty God, and His promises are always true.

Love you all. Always remember: Shine Your Light! -ky♡

REFERENCES

1. Spurgeon, C. H. (1876, March 19). *Feeble Faith Appealing to a Strong Saviour.* The Spurgeon Center. Retrieved May 17, 2022, from https://www.spurgeon.org/resource-library/sermons/feeble-faith-appealing-to-a-strong-saviour/#flipbook/

2. Williams, Zach. "Fear is a Liar." *Spotify.* https://open.spotify.com/track/6Z85UCEueQcgSyChl rEu5G

3. Scripture quotations are taken from the Holy Bible, New Living Translation, copyright ©1996, 2004, 2015 by Tyndale House Foundation. Used by permission of Tyndale House Publishers, Carol Stream, Illinois 60188. All rights reserved.